Interborough Pharaoh
Poems

Interborough Pharaoh
poems

Chavy Delgado

UNDR
GRND

The Underground Publishing House, N.Y.

For inquiries, publication information, or permission
to reproduce selections from this book, write to: The
Underground, College of Mount Saint Vincent,
6301 Riverdale Avenue, Bronx, NY 10471, or e-mail:
theunderground@mountsaintvincent.edu

ISBN: 978-1-940068-02-2

Printed in the United States of America

CONTENTS

I have a friend who thinks all good ideas come from riding on a train. "It's something about the noise they make," he said in his soft-like-rain voice, and I laughed because the sound of a train is beautiful, but my ideas aren't.

— ankhesenamun

EVOLUTION (Life struggles)

What struggles have I lived through other than wiggling out of bed?

Being put on the spot, I can't really think of them.
But I know my soul has been torn. I know my heart has been broken.
I know that I've lain in bed and cried. I know that I've looked at the sky
  and yelled.

So what's my problem?!
Why can't I think of my struggles?
Why am I wasting time trying to remember?

Maybe I'm stronger than I thought.
Maybe as a human being I have surpassed those struggles.
I have surpassed.
I'm ready for my next batch.

I'm ready to be stronger than I am at this moment,
Ready to evolve.

VELVET

I touch your skin and to my surprise
It is I who gets goosebumps.
How is this so? How could this be...
Your skin soft as velvet while I'm a tree?
How accurate to say that you own my leaves,
Your smile is my sun, all you do is radiate me.

As you feed my soul with your life-giving kiss,
I realize that I can never be without thee:
Soft velvet skin,
Beautiful, radiant smile,
And that kiss that saved me from myself.

HOWL WITH ME (The Moon)

All of the moments that I have been awake in my life: Night.
I was born in the dark, I spoke in the dark, I learned in the dark,
My only companion: the Moon.
At some point in my life I realized how far the Moon was from me.

Then I realized that I had to use all my strength to have my voice
    reach the Moon and the stars beyond.
Then I realized that I might not have enough strength to reach those
    directly around me.

Then I howled…
I used the remainder of my strength to give a final plea.

The Moon glared back.

The Moon has been my companion.
I have never been alone,
And I welcome those who found the Moon as comfort
    (we are the same creature):
Howl with me.

TEACH

You are your own greatest teacher.
Prove me wrong and I'll give you a star of gold.
Never forget the first lesson you taught yourself.

What am I saying?! You already knew that.

The words I am writing are for you. They always have been.
I am a teacher myself.
More importantly, I am a learner.
So please, *teach* me your most important lesson.
I am a gentleman with time to spare and a true hunger for you.

HOPE (Happiness that you've found tonight)

Tonight:
Drinking with family, I've realized:
I am important.

I am important in the eyes of my family.
(As all children should be.)

I have to use every inch of my being to fight.
My soul, my heart, the muscles in *my* body…
Because that is what was done before me.

What was done before me is not a blueprint.
What was done before me is a foundation that I have to build on.

PHARAOH DELGADO

What does it take to make gold?
Fuck the physical world...
I'm curious about the soul. I'm curious about the heart.
How do I make my actions gold?

At this moment, I wonder what is truly worth value...
Is it the gold on my fingers, neck, or wrist?
Or is it the acts that I create?
Is it the love that I show?

I want to live forever, and like a Pharaoh, I will take my gold with me.
But what do I leave with the people?

LIFE (Getting lost in a city you know nothing about)

I didn't think hard, I thought quick.
I jumped on a train.
I'm getting lost in a city I know nothing about.

Nothing has changed.
That is what all of life has been:
Getting lost.

BREATHE DEEP (The last dream you remember)

I'm going to live forever...

And I ask you to join me, because the only fear I have is being alone.
I fear not being able to share my wealth.

What if I wake up to luxury?
What if I wake up to a cement ground?

Then... what if I wake up to a world that knows my name?
A world that knows my purpose.

Then I woke up
And thought... what is my purpose?

COMFORT (Your favorite smell)

I have read that smell triggers memory better than any other sense.
I have experienced that smell triggers memory better than any other sense.
Moments in which I was nonchalant, moments in which I was running
on instinct alone,
Moments in which I forgot myself... Moments in which you were
not there!
Your scarf appeared and your scarf was scented just like what I
remembered.
Then I remembered: You broke and I stayed myself, I stayed strong.
That is my greatest conquest, that I am stronger than what made me
weak.

WHAT? (Alcohol and its effects)

How is it that I can feel so numb and so emotional at the same time?
There have been moments I wish I didn't have to remember!
And I can't remember if those moments where influenced by my soul
   or the 80-proof whiskey that I took hours before.
What am I to do?! I fell in love with how you make me feel.
I fell in love with not having to care. I fell in love with not being
   myself.

Yet isn't your effect making me who I truly am at heart?
I've heard in my life, "Drunk thoughts speak sober words."

Fuck that. I've said ridiculous shit while I was drunk.

Shit… what if I was thinking it before I said.

IT'S YOURS, NOT MINE (Long hair)

Growing out my hair has been so much fun.
I still remember the start of its growth
While I was young, dumb, and stung (shout outs to *Say Anything*).
Enough about me… let me think about you.
How long and how strong your hair has become.
I am thinking and dreaming of feeling each strand.

Allow me some rest,
For I cannot stand a beautiful girl with long hair.

SPUD (Potato)

Ima eat you, spud.
Cook ya, maybe boil ya.
Forget it, you getting fried, boy.
Au revoir.

GOOD QUESTION?

I asked myself, "Why?"
Why am I doing what I'm doing?

There's a simple answer.
I do my shit to die, you do your shit knowing you're going to die.
We are the same person.
Who is right? Who is wrong?

What a strange thought.
What a strange life.

TINY LITTLE THING THAT I CAN'T SEE, WITHOUT YOU I'D BE NOTHING (Microscopic life)

It is interesting to think that we all work together on a similar level to cells. We all have different roles to play in life, in this world.
Just as cells travel through veins and arteries, we travel through roads and freeways.
It's funny to think how much everything is all related, yet there is such a disdain toward what one may find different.

No matter how different any being is, there is an ultimate similarity between how they work and how we work.

GONE (Live to die)

I was born… Given life.
Now comes the middle… Living life.
How long is the middle…? I don't even know.
Dead.

LOVER OF TRAGEDY (Your best night)

I am a lover of emotions.
The more emotion I feel, the more alive I feel.

My best night is the night I felt the most emotion.
My best night is the night that I regret the most.

EVERYDAY (Your true love)

The truest love I was ever taught is the love all humans need.
The truest love I was ever taught is a constant love.

I love every day.
My true love is the smile on people's faces, after a joke, after an act
   of kindness…
After giving myself completely.

LOOK AND LISTEN (My best advice)

Sometimes we forget that there are people living among us who are living the same life.

MY FAMILY GOT A FISH DEALER

It's true: A guy just sells my family fish in dimes and dubs.
I don't even think it's legal.

I hate fish.

PATHETIC (Penguins)

Can I live in snow, naked and without thought?
I can try.

Catch me dancing on my grave, my whole body frostbitten.
Catch me reincarnated in Antarctica.

GOODBYE, DARLING (Being in love with someone who used to be your best friend but isn't anymore because you know you were never good enough for her)

I used to be so proud of who I was. Then I met you.
You gave me value. That's something I could never do for myself.
When you made me feel whole, at that moment I realized I'm in deep shit.
I realized that I could not make anyone feel complete. And with that, I realized you didn't know what you were doing.
So I left.

IT'S BEEN A WHILE (Not knowing how to accept love)

Oh my, here I am again.
You're talking to me daily… and my responses are… not what you want
  them to be.
What a fucking night.
All I want to do is talk to you and quit because I am just too scared.
Just too scarred.
I'm not ready, but I need this.
I just don't know how to accept this.

I KEEP TELLING MYSELF

I don't need another cigarette.
I don't need another moment awake.
I don't need another moment thinking of you.

I NEVER

I never want to love someone as much as my grandmother
   loves my grandfather.
It's been 7 years and I've never seen anyone as lonely as her.
I never want anyone to love me that much either.
But I'm afraid it's too late.
Cursed since birth.
Yeah, maybe I'm lucky. Whatever…
I just never want to hurt anyone.
But I'm afraid I'm too late.

NEVER ON TOP

Even a shark has predators.

LONELY

My brother told me to write every night.
My brother was right.

My brother told me to use all my might,
All my might to reach the highest height.

My brother told me, "Relax, stop being so tight."
I told my brother, "All right."

I am an only child.

WHY? (World manipulated by humans)

Dominance....
Have I deserved it?
I gave you life, yet you destroy me.
Is it poetic to die from what you've created?

CRUMBS

I love the beach. I feel like it is one of the most beautiful places we
   have on this planet. You know what's a big contribution to that?
The sand.
You know what the sand is?
The crumbs of once great rocks.
Would everything that crumbles be part of something more beautiful?

WHAT A THOUGHT...

Never have I ever
Fallen in love at first sight.

Shit… love at first contact,
It's all right.
I'll just brush it off.

ORANGES

Freshly squeezed on the table.
I drank this all week just 'cause you squeezed it.
Now let me sip something else after I squeezed it.

I DREAM OF PIZZA (Lack of pizza)

Late at night, when the cool cats are up,
I ponder and hope for something rare and rich.
I scream and I pray, I pray and I scream for my dreams to come true.
For I dream of pizza.
This dream, she is pure.
My body aches, my heart she quakes,
All for a fucking slice.

I BOUGHT A SIX PACK

Hahaha,
I bought a six pack.
Here's the funny part: I'm not worried about:
Sleep right now, school in the morning, work in the afternoon,
The cough I have, the headache Ima get, the shit I have to do,
The bills I gotta pay, money I have to save.
Don't expect an excuse from me. I'll give you a solid answer.
Hahahahahahahahahahaha.

FUNGUS

What is that smell?
Oh dear… it's my shoes.
Now I'll bury them, eat what comes in June.
By myself or without you.

USED

I walked into this situation. All I know is that we're both smoking
   a cigarette
And you're trying to sit on my lap because all the seats are taken.
Truth be told, I'll be a chair for a bit. But I won't stick around long
   enough for you to get comfortable.
I've been rode too many times.
I need an oil change.
I need a change.

PEEPING TOM

I'm naked.
Only because I saw you last week, looking at me change.
And honestly… I'm okay with it. Just don't touch.
You can look… And after a while, maybe you can touch.
Just make sure I'm okay with it.
Don't touch yet…
Just peep.

FREE FALLING

I just jumped off a cliff.
Bye.

THAT'S WHAT POETRY IS, A BUNCH OF CONFLICTED THOUGHTS

CREATE

Define creation, think it through real good.
Now tell me, are you a creator?
Are you a god amongst your peers?
Are you a loner?

I am a creator.
I've built a mountain, and though it is only theoretical, it will last
  beyond my lifetime.
I look down from my mountain and see nothing.

I look on my level and I see you all.
We are all creators of beauty and malice.
Our mountains beneath us are only what we've built them up to be.

I am only stating the obvious.

THE WHISKEY NEVER WATERS DOWN

Pour some whiskey in my glass,
Throw some rocks.

Drink it quick.

The whiskey never waters down.
Not in my cup.

OVER LIVING

I have lived
Long enough to try,
Long enough to cry.
I have lived my limit.
I don't want to stop.

HEY, MAN

I could do it. I can go out there.
Trust me. I'm good.

"Nah, you're not good."
Yeah, I am.
"Okay, see you later."

I know you're not good. I just let you go.
I wonder, who is crazy, me who let you go,
Or you who left, knowing you needed me?

BEAUTIFUL CURSE (One individual seeing color in a black and white world)

Is it truly a blessing to be different?
No one else looks at that sky as I look at it.
And no one else looks into your eyes as I do.
I am frightened by the sun
Just as I am frightened by the color your face turns when you're upset.

Is no one seeing what I am seeing?
Is this a disability, a curse, or a blessing?

Wait...
It's a little bit of all three
and then some.

CANDY FROM A GROWN-ASS MAN (Government stealing from people)

We all love candy. This much is true.
I love candy maybe a little more than you.
Now watch me go, get a degree,
And with said degree, steal all the candy from thee.
Once I steal it, I will be all for me.

Maybe I'll trick you, share for a while.
But in the end, it will all be mine.
I'll give you big words, give you some hope
That your candy will return into your pockets.
Once you've been played a fool and seem not to notice,
I'll sucker punch ya and take what is mine.
I know you don't deserve it.

IN THE SKY (Grass)

It's funny how I feel closest to the sky as I lie on the grass.
Just give me some shade and some warmth and I'm ready to doze.
To go into a world that has been awaiting my arrival,
My dreams prepare because I am enlightened.
Before I enter my sweet slumber,
I take one more pull to continue to be heightened.

HOW HURT YOU MUST FEEL (Wasted potential)

How hurt you must feel to know that you have failed.
How hurt you must feel to know that you have lost,
To know that it was your entire fault,
To know that you were wired for success,
Yet your flaws caused disgrace.
Yet who you are isn't who you could have been.
At least in the end you'll feed the Earth and her trees.
At least in your death you can waste and not be useless.

WITHDRAWAL

I remember not being able to feel my feelings
And I miss that.
I miss that emptiness because now all that's there is you.

PLEASE

Don't look at me.
I really don't want you to realize I'm not looking at anything.
I don't want you to look my direction
Only because
I'm not there.

EMPTY FEELINGS

How can I feel so welcomed when a I walk into an empty house?
That's interesting...
Maybe it's because I am an empty person
With emotions that will mean nothing to you.

But I cannot say this fullheartedly
Because my empty feelings are what drive my soul,
The soul that isn't there.

Empty.

HAIRLESS CATS

How dear and pleasant it feels to rub my face against you and not have to worry about a burn in the morning.

DREAM

I am a dreamer.
I'm dreaming now I was dreaming a moment ago.
I stopped writing to dream.
I closed my eyes to dream.
I opened my heart to dream.

At some points I cannot separate my dreams from my future.
At some points I feel that fate exists.
At some points I feel free to choose any fate I decide.

With closed eyes and an open heart, I just have to feel my way around.
And if it be that my feelings are wrong, at least I followed my heart
For the whole journey in its entirety
For myself and every other dreamer on a journey.

MOST

Most of our generation love bread.
Most of our generation love alcohol.
I'm pretty sure the good book mentions bread and wine... many times.
I am pretty sure a life revolved around bread and wine is a life to live.

Now, what do we fill the rest of the gaps with...?
I say giving. Some say taking. Some say waiting.
I say let's multiply the bread and wine we have. I say let's share.
I say let's write a good book.

I TEND TO FORGET I DON'T HAVE A REAL FAMILY

I wish more people would love wholeheartedly.

I TEND TO FORGET I AM AN ACTOR

At times,
I tend to forget I am an actor.
I believe myself at times.
It's a funny thought.
The funniest:
I'll break the 4th wall with my audience before I ever break it with
    myself.

CHINESE FOOD

If you don't have Orange Chicken
Don't answer my phone call.
If you don't have Pork Fried Rice
What kind of Chinese food spot are you running?

TAKE MY HAT OFF!

I don't know where my head has been.

WINTER AIR

Winter air,
You're so inviting,
Much more inviting than the rest of my life.

WE

We are all poets and artists.
This is a generation of people who think freely,
A generation of minds that don't give a fuck.
Yet
We are easily molded.

I am easily molded.
I wish I was like a rock, staying the same in all my journeys.
Rock can still turn into sand.

Man, what?

TRAVELING

"Wake up, you idiot, you are going to be late for school again."
I felt it, just like I did every other time it was close to passing,
   the rusted painted metal passing through my home over my head,
   the train passed.
No one home,
No cooked meal.
When I was younger, it got to me.
But now, to be alone in the morning is a beautiful feeling.

My favorite part of my journey is the actual journey itself:
The Six train. I feel clarity amongst the loud sounds he makes.
I feel like I have a united family under its roof filled with complete
   strangers.
I look down from the train and I see the cars.
An accident along the highway.
Makes me jittery to even step in a car.

The train is there for me.

Months pass
Alone alone alone
Except for an inanimate object that shows "love" and "compassion"
To anyone who pays the fare (like a prostitute).

My old love was left behind... he was obsolete. But it is the duty of
   every son to leave behind his father, to make his own successful family.
MTA's greatest creation: Me. The train cars made me.

The earliest memory I own contains the Six train. I remember feeling
superior to it because I can talk, and one time while I was taunting it,
   it yelled back. That is when it earned my respect.
When I realized that I had no father, that I was a bastard, that the world's
   only purpose to me was to feel useless, he kept passing.
There are things in the world that are reliable.

BAD FORTUNE

What a strange week.
I lost my two front teeth.
That's the truth.
The cool thing about my luck? I'm only 7.
My teeth will grow back.
My luck will come back.

I HAD A DREAM

I had a dream earlier this week. All I was doing was lying in bed,
  texting an old friend.
I was happy.

IF I HAD ONE WISH IN THE WORLD

I'd wish that everyone without the ability to walk could walk.
Or I'd wish I knew all the secrets of the universe.
What would your wish be?

BUNNIES

As a child, I had a dream a couple of bunnies saved me from drowning. The dream seemed real and so did the rescue.

BEGINNING TO A NOVEL I STARTED YEARS AGO
(Excerpt)

He can run, he is strong, he is knowledgeable, he knows the flaws of the world, but he can't do a thing because his body is too weak. He goes back inside and grabs a pen, for he is overrun by emotions. He begins writing a book. This is the least he can do for mankind. He's ten pages into it. He has an appointment the next day and he needs his newfound strength. He goes to bed and is resting. The world is scared, for it has a true man on its dirt and this man will control humans, give them hope, and make them grow.

YOU ARE MY GREATEST PRIZE

Your eyes are perfect. Your soul aligned with mine makes me feel divine.
You are my goddess, whom I shall treasure.

Yet like all of man's treasures, at times you may feel belittled. Do not worry:
You are my greatest prize. I will cherish you with all my being.

The fire in your smile has wounded me.
I shall let it fester until I am purely infected with your love.

JUNE 22, 2007

Shit, I remember waking up to that phone call. It's been years, long years. I grew up without a father. *No,* honestly I had a father. It was you, Papito. You taught me to be fair and honest, to be a caring person, and most importantly, to be compassionate and loving. You made me a man. But you left me so early. As a child, I dreamt of you teaching me how to drive. I dreamt of you being at my graduation.

Even when they took off your arm and you had only one left, you were still the strongest man I knew. You still drove, you still took care of the house, you still loved me and our family. You weren't my real grandfather, but I don't care. You're my old man, my dad, my teacher, and I wish you were still here. I still have so much to learn from you.

You left me with some task. You asked me to look after your home, you asked me to look after your wife, you asked me to look after your family, you asked me to become someone important, *you asked me to get an education.* You asked me for so much, but I will live my life to please you. Thank you for being my influence. Thank you for making me patient and understanding.

Papito, I love you. *Mi viejito, nada mi hace olividar de ti. Te amo con todo mi corazon y alma.* One day I will be a fraction of the man you are. One day I will be strong and have my own family, and one day I will teach my little ones what you taught me. I miss your laugh and how powerful it was. I miss how your laugh made me smile and how it warmed my soul.

You raised me since birth. You are my dream. You are the reason that I have any good in me.

I wouldn't be Chavy Alexy Delgado without Manuel "Papito" Mero.

BLANK (Anything)

The worse sin is doing nothing with your life.

www.ingramcontent.com/pod-product-compliance
Lightning Source LLC
Chambersburg PA
CBHW021219020426

42331CB00003B/375